The
Great Date Wait
and Other Hazards

Distributed by
CHOICE BOOKS
Salunga, Pa. 17538
We welcome your response

The Great Date Wait

and Other Hazards

William L. Coleman

BETHANY HOUSE PUBLISHERS
MINNEAPOLIS, MN 55438

Scripture verses marked TLB are taken from The Living Bible, copyright 1971 by Tyndale House Publishers, Wheaton, Ill. Used by permission.

Photos by: Kevin Dekrey, Dick Easterday, and Gary Johnson.

Published by Bethany House Publishers
A division of Bethany Fellowship, Inc.
6820 Auto Club Road, Minneapolis, Minnesota 55438

Printed in the United States of America

Library of Congress Cataloging in Publication Data

Coleman, William L.
    The great date wait, and other hazards.

    1. Youth—Prayer-books and devotions—English.
2. Family—Prayer-books and devotions—English.   I. Title.
BV4850.C565   248.8'3   82-1233
ISBN 0-87123-348-7 (pbk.)   AACR2

About the Author

WILLIAM COLEMAN is becoming increasingly well known as a gifted writer and author. He has written a number of devotionals for families with young children (listed at the back of this book). He has also begun an adventure-mystery series for ages 8-15, of which three titles are available. This is his first teen devotional.

Coleman is a graduate of the Washington Bible College in Washington, D.C., and Grace Theological Seminary in Winona Lake, Indiana. He has pastored three churches and he is a Staley Foundation lecturer. His articles have appeared in several well-known evangelical magazines. He lives in Aurora, Nebraska with his wife and three children.

Table of Contents

People Are Fun!

Life would be a dry cracker if it were not for people. Friends, new faces, and a few relatives sprinkled here and there are a big part of what makes life exciting.

People are also a good challenge. How do we keep an old friendship fresh? How do we accept a date, how do we get one, and what do we do if there is no date? How do we react when the person sitting next to us is a bigger pain than a pinched nerve?

All of us need a few suggestions and a guideline or two. I hope you will let God be part of your relationships.

William L. Coleman
Aurora, Nebraska

The First Date

Dear Mary,

It's a great time! Enjoy it! Your first date will always have a special place in your memory.

When he called to ask you for a date, we all acted stunned, like we didn't know what was happening. Now we realize our daughter is maturing before our very eyes. You are taking a big social step and we weren't entirely ready for it.

Thanks for playing it cool. You asked him to call back while you checked with your parents. You handled it calmly even though it has come like Christmas in July!

There was no doubt in my mind that I should say yes, but I really appreciated your thoughtfulness. You didn't tell him yes, and *then* check with us. Cool, calm, respectful. If you had told me you had already said yes, my reaction would have been negative, even hostile. Thanks for letting me down easy.

First dates are harder on fathers than on daughters. It seemed natural to you. You could hardly wait for the day when you would begin dating. But it was like pulling a tooth for a dad. No matter what happens, it will never be the same again. No matter what the future holds, we can never put you back into the same package again. You are freer than you have ever been before.

A dad feels like a trapeze artist. He wants to jump to the swing bar but hates to leave the platform. Thanks for taking me gently.

Some of our friends will keep their daughters from dating until they are sixteen. That may be all right for them. I have thought about it a lot before now, but decided that hat didn't fit either one of us. Besides, I reasoned, why make a big fuss about her age when maybe no one will ask her out anyway?

There is nothing magic about age. Sixteen won't make

you a young lady. He asked. You seemed ready. I said yes. It all seemed so simple. So natural.

But, after I said yes, a million questions popped into my mind. (And at least a thousand doubts.)

It was a bit like signing a document and *then* asking what it said. That's when the facts began to surface. They didn't seem big to you, but they were new to me!

I didn't realize he was a senior! (I thought—a senior with *my* little girl?) I didn't realize your close friends had not dated. (I thought you were the slow starter.)

Maybe these are things I didn't need to know. Young people usually understand their world best.

There are many things I would like to have said at the time, as I look back. But you don't think of everything on the spur of the moment.

Instead, I want you to remember four things. (I'll list them here for now, and for future reference.)

First, I have set a time to be home. It's a ball-park figure; you can come in a little later if you need to. But, you can also use the curfew to come home promptly if you want to terminate the date.

Second, what do you talk about? I suggest you aim at what interests your date. It's a good rule with any friend.

Third, eat lightly. The date will cost him a gold tooth as it is!

Fourth, don't feel any need to become physical. Some couples think they have to kiss good night to show they had a good time. Others think they have to go even further. Don't fall for that trap. The less physical you are the better you will feel about yourself, and about your relationship.

Who can say when you might have another date? Who knows when you will even want one? But this one will be great. Have a terrific first date!

"It's a wonderful thing to be alive" (Eccles. 11:7, TLB).

Love,
Dad

Something to Think About:

1. If you have dated, what was your first date like?
2. Do you recommend dating a lot, a little, or not at all?
3. How do your friends feel about dating?

Nobody's Better

Dear Mary,

Who are the most important people you know? You may automatically think of a president, or a scientist, or an athlete because we generally treat them as special individuals. They seem to get a great deal of attention, and often a sizable amount of money, too.

These are the guidelines we frequently use to measure someone's worth in our society: fame and wealth.

It's a shame, because we lose sight of the *real* person. An individual does not consist of what he has, or what his skills are.

People who are financially poor are often wonderful human beings. Young people restricted to wheelchairs can be as great as anyone who ever crosses a finish line at the Olympics. One-fourth of the people in the United States are handicapped in some way. Each one of us is as important as any king could be.

When award assemblies are held, students are asked to stand and receive their awards for special accomplishments. You have received a number of these and we are extremely proud. However, no award makes you better. No lack of an award makes you worse. You are a great person either way.

I hope you will continue to pick friends on the same basis. What is really important is the person, and not what he does.

Try never to hold a prejudice against the poor. God loves them very much. Try never to develop a prejudice against the rich. God loves them very much, also.

Sometimes it is hard to like people who are highly gifted.

All of us are human beings. Every person hurts at sometime or another, but often we are afraid to show it.

Mary, you are no better than anyone else. You are also no less. You are a unique individual. That makes it possible for us to accept ourselves. It also makes it possible to open our arms and hearts and help others.

Walk through life with your head up. You are everyone's equal. But, you are also everyone's servant.

"If a man comes into your church dressed in expensive clothes and with valuable gold rings on his fingers, and at the same moment another man comes in who is poor and dressed in threadbare clothes, and you make a lot of fuss over the rich man and give him the best seat in the house and say to the poor man, 'You can stand over there if you like, or else sit on the floor'—well, judging a man by his wealth shows that you are guided by wrong motives" (James 2:2-4, TLB).

Love,
Dad

Something to Think About:

1. What are some prejudices in your community?
2. Do you try to be friends with people of all kinds of backgrounds and capabilities?
3. Have you ever befriended someone who especially needed a friend? How did it work out?

Sparkling Eyes

Dear June,

You have an excellent quality and I hope you will keep it all your life. You know how to make someone's eye sparkle by telling them "thank you."

That is one of the greatest gifts in the world, and it's free! Hand it out often. Spread it around generously.

How did you feel when your music teacher gave you that beautiful music box? She wanted to thank you for playing the piano at the concert. Remember the surprise! Remember the feeling of being appreciated? Remember all of this and keep passing those same feelings on to other people.

Some people have thankless jobs. It seems like the only time they hear about their work is when somebody complains. School principals, policemen, custodians, newspaper editors, and teachers are merely the beginning of the long list.

When you hug your mother and tell her thank you, it lights up her day. It means someone noticed. Someone realized it took work to do what she did. (It also makes her want to do more.)

Brothers and sisters light up when they are appreciated. Thank you's seem to mellow them and make them more loving.

Sending thank-you notes to people on your paper route is another terrific idea of yours. You don't just grab a tip or gift and run. That note in the mail is a certain eye-sparkler. They know you appreciate their thoughtfulness. That makes them want to continue to be kind.

None of us really lives unto himself. We affect the people around us. When we growl and stomp through the day, our attitude makes others feel low and grouchy too. When we are pleasant and cheerful and grateful, we perk up the lives of others we meet.

Thankfulness is a priceless attitude, and all of us can have it. You have set a good example. Thanks.

Always give thanks for everything to our God and Father in the name of the Lord Jesus Christ (Eph. 5:20).

Love,
Dad

Something to Think About:

1. Name one happy surprise you've had.
2. Do you like to reward others?
3. Can you think of someone who probably seldom gets thanked? Can you do something for that person?

Teenagers Are Terrific

Dear Jim,

There was a terrible accident not too far from here and two men were trapped in a flaming car. Five people saw the inferno and rushed to see if they could help. Fire had engulfed the vehicle and the situation looked hopeless. At considerable risk to themselves, the five grabbed the doors and pulled the two men outside. What is amazing is that the five young men were teenagers.

Some young people get a bad name because they do a few reckless or thoughtless things. But, many more do admirable things, and they should be commended.

There is a hospital in Omaha which has been flooded with volunteer workers. They now have 130 teenage boys and girls who give their time to assist patients. Volunteers have been coming for over ten years. The hospital does not have to recruit extra help. Just by word-of-mouth their ranks have been kept up.

Who would ever think that teenagers would give up treasured leisure time to work in a hospital? Teenagers are terrific people!

I've always been impressed with the young people who spend their summers working with children in Appalachia. Many families there have very little. Each year, teenagers go there to help and show that they care. They have a great time, but it also means sacrifice. It's scary to go into a new situation not knowing what the people are like, or how you will be accepted.

Many teenagers live a steady, good life. They have a good time, they accept responsibility, and they get along great with others.

Young people have much to learn, but they also have much to teach. We can all learn from their lives.

"Don't let anyone think little of you because you are

young. Be their ideal; let them follow the way you teach and live; be a pattern for them in your love, your faith, and your clean thoughts" (1 Tim. 4:12, TLB).

Love,
Dad

Something to Think About:

1. Can you think of a project you could do for someone else?
2. Has your family ever done a project for somebody who needed help?
3. Can you think of some things Christ would do if He were in your neighborhood?

A Better Idea!

Dear Mary,

"Marriage is so much better than dating!" I've heard this from many adults. Dating is fun, but it is an uneasy game to play.

A girl sits around waiting for some guy to call her. Meanwhile, she plays mental games. She tells herself there are boys who would like to call her but they are afraid. (She's probably right.) Another tells herself the boys are too bashful to call a girl as pretty as she. (She could be right.)

At the same time she has a subtle fear. What if some creep calls? She hopes the kid in ninth grade who's been eyeing her, doesn't bother.

Dating is a nerve-wracking ordeal.

The boys are going through a similar agony. They have chewed their fingernails down to their sweatbands. Many want to invite the girl but are too scared to whistle.

It's a terrible experience for a guy. He has to stick his neck out for a girl to chop it off. If she turns him down, he feels like a rat.

If she says yes, his problems are almost as bad. Where would she enjoy going? How much will it cost? Does she expect him to kiss her? Questions shoot through his mind like a BB through a tin can.

There may be a better idea. It won't eliminate *all* the frustrations of dating, but it could help.

In the late twentieth century maybe we should have more girls asking boys out. Don't throw this letter away! Hear me out. A girl could simply say, "Would you like to go to a movie Friday? We could each pay our own way."

Society will not crumble. The Western world will not fold.

First, we have to remember dating is not a mating call. It is a social function—an opportunity to have a good time and get to know someone better. Once we remove dating

from the realm of great passion, many things are possible.

Some girls may believe it would be a good idea, but don't want to be so brash as to be the first to do it. Here is the solution.

Two girls who know each other fairly well should agree to do it. Each could ask a boy if he would like to go out for pizza Friday night. Each would pay his own way. With two of you doing it, you would feel more comfortable. If you did it a couple of times, few would consider it odd.

Make sure the boys are friends of yours! Everyone will know this date is no "love affair." Begin breaking the ice, and young people will be doing each other a tremendous favor.

Go on, Mary! I dare you.

Love,
Dad

Something to Think About:

1. Have you ever asked someone out? Explain.
2. How expensive does dating need to be where you live?
3. How do you ask someone out? By phone, in person, etc.?

Simple Self-respect

Dear Jim,

Paul was the kind of kid who didn't care. If he was thrown out of class for making a disturbance, that was all right. He wasn't doing very well in school anyway.

If Paul had to stay after school, that was fine. He didn't have anything to do or anyplace to go.

He was the kind of person who would break out windows, steal things off porches, or scratch up cars. Why not? Paul's life was dull. No one paid any attention to him. The best way to get some action going was to get into trouble.

All of us know at least one Paul, possibly several. They don't care about themselves. That's why they don't care about anyone else or anyone else's property.

It's tough to live when your life is empty. It's hard to live with yourself when you think you are useless.

All respect begins with self-respect. That's why it is important to like yourself and know you have abilities. If you feel good about yourself, you will feel free to help others instead of hurting them.

Sometime make a short list in your mind of all the things you do reasonably well.

You play a number of sports. You are an excellent friend. You handle your money carefully. You are an above-average student. You are considerate of other people. You are good with your hands.

The list could go on, but I don't want you to get big-headed! You can add more things on your own. All of us have talents and abilities. That is the way God made us. He created people who could do things.

Each gift you and I have has come from God. When we make our lists, we don't have to give ourselves all the credit. Hopefully we will become thankful to God.

The Bible puts it this way, "Every good gift and every perfect gift is from above" (James 1:17, KJV).

A mother recently said she had two gifted children. She didn't know what their gifts were yet, but she was sure they were gifted.

You have an advantage. You already know you have gifts. So don't feel inferior. And don't feel superior. Just be happy to be you. Be content with the gifts God has given you.

Love,
Dad

Something to Think About:

1. Name a talent you have.
2. If you are reading this as a family, name a talent of the one sitting next to you.
3. When was the last time you thanked God for a talent He has given you?

It Isn't Fair!

Dear Mary,

It isn't fair for a girl to have to sit home and wait for the telephone to ring. She is supposed to sit by the road like a flower expecting to be picked!

It must be a hopeless feeling. The guy you want to date never calls. The guy you would rather not does.

In my opinion it's a lousy system. Some girls become lonely, disappointed, and bitter about it. I've seen other girls who have become big-headed and proud because the "right" guy does call.

Don't let dating mess up your view of life. Dates do not make you a valuable, important person. A lack of dates does not mean you are worthless.

You already know that, but it's easy to forget. In our society we measure a person's value based on what he can do. "A" students are put on pedestals. Athletes are made national heroes. Homecoming queens are rated as goddesses.

By now you know how short-sighted that system is. You know what it's like to win. And when you take time to count your accomplishments and your friends, you feel a measure of success and security.

You also know what it's like to lose: the "C" that kept you out of Honor Society; the play try-out that didn't measure up.

Winning, losing, being selected, being overlooked—these are not the things that make a person valuable. Let me suggest three things that make you, or anyone, important.

First, you are extremely valuable because you are a human being. God created us. He is concerned about the sparrow, how much more about us.

"So God made man like his Maker. Like God did God make man; Man and maid did he make them" (Gen. 1:27, TLB). That makes us worthwhile.

Second, you are valuable because you are capable of loving people. Each friend, relative, or stranger you reach out to is evidence of your value. You add to their lives. You can soften their hurts and brighten their smiles.

If you were suddenly eliminated from the picture, an enormous gap would be left. People would be hurt, they would feel empty, they would cry, inside and out. They would feel that way because you are extremely important to many people.

Third, you are capable of receiving love. None of us lives unto himself. We must learn to receive as well as give. We can make others feel worthwhile by receiving what they have to offer us.

It's strange how we evaluate people. We say, "She is an important movie star," or "Scientists are important to our society," or "He's a valuable athlete."

It isn't fair. And it isn't true. People are important not for what they do or how they look or the recognition they receive.

A retarded child is valuable. The prisoner is valuable. The kid who flunked chemistry is valuable. The girl who can't shoot baskets is valuable.

Value has nothing to do with how often the phone rings. It has nothing to do with honor rolls.

You are loved—by God, your family, and your friends. Nothing could be more valuable than you, a unique individual.

Love,
Dad

Something to Think About:

1. Name five people who are valuable to you.
2. Name five people to whom you mean a great deal.
3. Think of some way to let a lonely person know he is valuable.

Keeping Your Word

Dear June,

Most of us talk too much. For some reason we feel we have to say something. It's almost as if silence was a green, fanged monster we had to fight off by constantly talking.

Because we talk too much, we also tend to promise too much. It may sound good at first. We promise to be one place, then we promise to be somewhere else. Before long we have promised to be more places than we can possibly be at one time.

Your word is one of your most valuable possessions. It can determine your reputation to others. When you give your word to someone, it should be as good as gold. If the value of your word drops, because you break it, your friends will lose confidence in you.

Make promises very carefully. Think before you speak. Don't promise something you aren't sure you can carry out.

If you must break your word, because of an accident or a conflict, you will be smart to go to the person as soon as possible and explain your problem. That's one way to keep the value of your word.

Someone commented recently to me, "Ed told me he would be here this morning, but I knew he wouldn't. Ed means well but he seldom shows up."

It's a shame, but Ed's word isn't worth a nickel. In his heart he probably wants to help, but somehow his body doesn't get into gear.

No one wants the label *undependable*. It doesn't speak well of him and it soon gives him a poor reputation.

Fortunately, you are off to a good start by keeping your word. In your jobs of delivering papers and mowing lawns, you have proven how dependable you are. If you tell someone you will take care of it, he can consider it done.

Your word has grown in worth. Keep it that way.

"Say just a simple, 'Yes, I will' or 'No, I won't.' Your word is enough. To strengthen your promise with a vow shows that something is wrong" (Matt. 5:37, TLB).

Love,
Dad

Something to Think About:

1. Have you ever promised something you couldn't carry out? What did you do about it?
2. Have you had someone break a promise to you? How did you feel?
3. Do you ever make quick promises just so you won't be bothered anymore?

A Balanced Outlook

Dear Mary,

Sometimes high-school dating is rated far too high. It's fun, but generally exaggerated. Dating is not the great pursuit of life. Life goes on with amazing ease without one high-school date.

Speaking as a has-been adult, I don't expect you to believe me. The very thought of dating sounds like rhapsody. Most girls think it is the ultimate in acceptance.

Dating can be great. But, as I said, its importance is tremendously exaggerated. Young people who complete high school without ever going on a date manage to survive very well. Their lives are still filled with excitment and meaning. Dating and marriage may come later. A full life—and no high-school dates! It happens all the time.

In fact, most high-school students don't date regularly. Many do not date at all. Only in movies and dreams do we imagine every young person with arms draped around each other in perfect contentment.

It's a myth—a fraud. Dating can be a good part of life, but it is not essential. It is far from the apex of youth. Enjoy dating for what it is, but don't inflate its importance.

The smart young person looks straight ahead. He involves himself in hobbies, sports, sets goals, accomplishes things. Dating is a sideline. Smart people don't let dating become mainline.

Too many girls waste time sulking over their lack of dates. They allow it to bend their personalities into miserable twists. Before long they doubt their self-worth. They begin to think they are rejected. Soaked in self-pity, they become withdrawn.

The odds against dating are enormous. Most of the boys you know are lanky, social misfits. Teenage boys tend to be uncomfortable near femininity. They may think they are in control, but usually they are as awkward as a bricklayer at a cooking contest.

Since boys mature late, they often date late. This leaves anxious teenage girls chewing their nails. Forget it. High-school dating isn't worth the agony. If it comes, enjoy it. If it doesn't, don't let it streak your mascara.

Suppose, just suppose, you never date anyone from now until you begin to date the man you marry. In the long run, what difference will it make?

A teenage girl told me she hoped marriage would be more fun than dating. It really is.

I hope I don't take any of the shine off dating. It can be tremendous fun. But don't let it get out of balance. Dating is only a *part* of life, and not a large part at that.

God's plan for your life and mine is full and complete.

Love,
Dad

Something to Think About:

1. Would you rather go out with a group of boys, a group of girls, a mixed group, or a single date?
2. Do most of your friends date?
3. How important do you think dating is?

Dare to Be Different

Dear Jim,

When we were kids we used to stand on the heat grates at the Library of Congress to keep warm. On a dark, dreary day no one paid much attention to a bunch of boys on the lawn.

As we stood there we would pass cigarettes around. We didn't have many so we would take turns puffing on them.

Why did we huddle there like alcoholics passing a bottle? The smokes weren't that great. None of us really knew how to smoke. We would drag in, then hack, cough and spit out white clouds.

You had to be careful because some guy would always try to "cuff" you. We had cuffs on our trousers, and when you weren't looking someone would put a cigarette in your cuff. Soon you would notice smoke rising by your side and you would fight frantically to get the tiny torch out of your clothes.

It's safe to say that not one of us who met there enjoyed smoking. It's hard to get much fun out of breathing smoke and hot air. But still we did it. And you know why we did it? We wanted to be like everyone else.

Not many of us dared to be different then. From what I see, it is the same story with young people today. We all get sucked into some dumb thing because we want to conform and be accepted—we need to fit in.

"We" is the correct usage here. Adults don't do much better at choosing the right way. There is pressure all our lives to merely give in and be like others. The more independent thinkers seem to be little children and old ladies.

It isn't all bad to be like others. You don't want to wear swimming trunks to school just because everyone else is wearing trousers. You don't want to drink from a saucer because everyone else uses cups.

However, there are some times when you definitely want to be your own man. You don't want to be led around by the nose to do things you really don't think are right.

You have a high Christian standard of living. Don't let anyone steal it away from you. Sometimes being different is the better way to go.

"Don't copy the behavior and customs of this world, but be a new and different person with a fresh newness in all you do and think. Then you will learn from your own experience how his ways will really satisfy you" (Rom. 12:2, TLB).

Love,
Dad

Something to Think About:

1. What percentage of students in your high school smoke?
2. Why do people smoke?
3. Do you think smoking is a smart thing to do?

The Meaning of Meals

Dear Mary,

Our world is changing fast and there aren't many traditions that will last. Each family will have to strive for its own individual way of life.

It's okay; we don't want to live in the past. Reach out for new and different things.

However, there is one part of the past I would really recommend you keep. If at all possible, try to gather your family around at least one meal a day, preferably your evening meal.

It might seem like a strange request, but there is a good reason. If your family is to be strong, it must find times to communicate. If you are to communicate together, there must be a time when all of you sit down. Mealtime is excellent for bringing everyone together at once.

Eating can be done buffet-style part of the time, food can be placed on a table, and everyone can eat when he wants to, and where he wants to, but sit-down meals are important because they allow people to share. Opinions, values, concerns, laughs, and ideas can be tossed around. We can find out how we feel and what we think is important.

The University of Nebraska took a national survey of strong families. They discovered that most strong families gather together at a mealtime. They considered this time important and made it a priority.

It's a busy life. Your family could be even busier than ours. It's a choice you and your husband will have to make, but give mealtime a strong consideration.

You are gentle and thoughtful, so I know you will never make mealtime a routine time. Make it uplifting, a time for sharing and encouragement. I predict they will be some of the happiest times for your family.

In the process of sharing, you can help your family grow in their faith in God and Jesus Christ.

Love,
Dad

Something to Think About:

1. Does your family have one meal together every day?
2. How could it be improved? What do you like about it?
3. Do you think your family is too strict about making the whole family be together at mealtime?

Laugh at Yourself

Dear June,

Some figures have come across my desk which show that cheating among students is on the rise. The students who are cheating in these cases are not junior- or senior-high students. The mushrooming problem is among college students.

They are supposed to be mature, young adults preparing to become our community leaders. How can they stoop so low as to cheat on a test?

Two students were paid to take tests for other students. One person was caught trying to steal the test from a faculty office. Others were smuggling notes into the exam room.

When asked why they chose to cheat, many of the students said they felt terrible pressure to get high grades. Their future in graduate school or in getting a job depended on how well they did.

Even before they were caught, these must have been sad people. They thought their grades had to be the very top or they would be rejected.

They took life too seriously. If they had gotten a C or a D, they would have felt their life was over. It's too bad they couldn't laugh at themselves and go on.

Remember the day Mary got a C in biology and missed the honor roll? Her eyes were filled with tears and I know her heart felt choked tight.

But Mary learned from that grade. She snapped back and went to work. Her life wasn't wrecked; it wasn't even dented. She came back and worked harder. Now she can look at that grade and laugh instead of cry.

Mature people don't have to cheat to keep up. Only hard work merits a good grade. You can come in fifth in the spelling contest and not throw a fit, or come in twelfth in a sack race and not think life is over.

Not everything in life is funny but many things are. We should learn to laugh at ourselves. If we take ourselves too seriously, we can end up with ulcers, a sour personality, or cheating on a test.

I imagine, and I can only imagine, that God must look at us every once in a while and burst out laughing.

"There is a time to laugh" (Eccles. 3:4, TLB).

Love,
Dad

Something to Think About:

1. Can you laugh when you goof up?
2. Do you know anyone who is a perfectionist and can't laugh at himself?
3. When you fail do you learn from your mistake?

Going in Groups

Dear Mary,

You have a terrific group of friends. There isn't one of them who doesn't seem like a nice person. You have had good times together and built some good memories.

When you go out with that crowd for the evening, it's easy for us to relax. All of them have been over to the house, and we have gotten to know them.

That's a good practice. When parents meet young people, it helps take the tension away. We don't know all the mischief you might try, but we feel assured you all mean well. You get a silver star for a smart move.

Groups are a good idea. There is no hurry to pair off when you don't want to. You can enjoy a variety of personalities and learn from each other.

When you want to go out for pizza or go skating, you dig up a carload. You laugh a lot, tease each other, and have a great time.

Sometime when you are thanking God for the things that count, remember to include your group. There are many who have no such collection of friends and they spend too much time alone. Others get wrapped into the wrong package of friends and later are sorry.

Your group seems like such a healthy combination. They lift each other up, set good examples, and encourage each other to do better.

Other groups are like an octopus. They reach out, squeeze, strangle and drag people down. Always down and never up.

There was a terrific girl in our high school who drifted into a group. She wanted to fit in. The further she slid into the group the more it squeezed and demanded.

Soon her personality began to change. Like a chameleon she soon matched her surroundings. Before long this great girl turned into a sarcastic, crude, difficult person.

We all tend to become like the group around us. Your

friends become more like you and you soon resemble them.

Every day that your group does something good, intelligent, and sane, thank God for them. Every time they are tempted to do something dumb or strange, gently help bring them back to reality.

A group of friends is one of the real prizes in life. Treat that treasure with great care.

When Paul thought about his close friends he wrote:

"I thank God upon every remembrance of you" (Phil. 1:3, KJV).

Love,
Dad

Something to Think About:

1. What is the best part of belonging to a group?
2. Name a few friends you are thankful for.
3. Do your parents know the members of your group?
4. In what ways does your group help you?

Asking Her Out

Dear Jim,

Girls think boys have it made. They believe a boy can ask any girl out he wants to and he's in perfect control.

If girls could only know what guys go through. In the first place, most guys don't know how to ask a girl for a date. "What do I say? Do I call them, or meet them in the hall?"

The second big fear is being turned down. Rejection makes you feel really lousy. Who wants to be told "no"?

As if these were not enough to frighten him, why does anyone want to go out with a girl anyway? If you are not used to being alone with her, it's hard to know what to say!

Most girls feel more comfortable in social settings than boys. Guys would rather snag fly balls or put night crawlers on hooks.

As boys get older, the pressure becomes greater to take a girl out. Some of it is social pressure and some is because he really wants to.

I'm not trying to get you to date. Only date *when* you want to and *if* you want to. However, when you feel ready a few suggestions might come in handy. Bounce them around and see what you think.

Remember that most girls will *not* turn you down. They would enjoy a good evening out just as much as you would. Don't act too seriously, and they will probably accept another date.

Ask her face to face if you can. That is the friendliest way. Be friendly but direct. Give the girl the facts in a warm way—where you will go, what you will do, and when you can have her home.

If she needs to think it over, and get permission from her parents, ask her when she can let you know. What do you do if she turns you down? Accept it politely, and ask someone else. The world won't end. Keep cool.

Rejection is worth the risk: most of the time you will be a winner.

Love,
Dad

Something to Think About:

1. Have you ever asked someone out and been turned down? How did you feel?
2. When there is a school event, do you want to date, or are you happier in a group?

Brothers and Sisters

Dear Mary,

Yesterday I saw the neatest scrapbook. A clever sister began putting it together four years ago so she could surprise her brother. The book was filled with interesting pictures, articles from the school paper, school and church bulletins. She silently collected all kinds of interesting "memories" for her younger brother.

The day he graduated from high school, she presented the scrapbook to him. What a terrific gift of love by someone who cared.

Caring for your younger brother or sister isn't out of style. Even though you knock heads once in a while, basically you are friends. There are times when you complain that they are "fire-breathing monsters," and sometimes they are. However, in the total picture it's great to have a brother or a sister.

Recently I attended a family seminar and heard about a survey taken of strong families. They found one of the best ingredients was that the family members appreciated each other. Brothers and sisters helped one another and paid each other compliments. They made other members of their family feel good about themselves.

Keep on doing a good job of that. You taught June how to read and how to play the piano. That made her feel great about herself as well as feeling good about her family. She knows she belongs and plays an important part.

If you have ever seen a jealous family, you know how harmful it can be. Brothers and sisters seem to be constantly trying to hurt one another. It is as if they feel better when they make someone else feel badly.

Your grades don't have to be higher than your brother's or sister's. Your talents and hobbies do not have to beat theirs. Each of us is a complete person. We are valuable because of who we are. We don't have to put someone else down to make ourselves feel significant.

Joseph and his brothers could not get along because they were busy being jealous (Gen. 37 ff.). They tried to kill Joseph and eventually sold him into slavery because they could not accept one another.

Cain and Abel could not accept each other so one brother murdered the other (Gen. 4).

The oldest child will usually set the pattern. When he or she is thoughtful, generous, and helpful it rubs off on the younger children.

Thanks for choosing to be kind. You affect everyone you meet by your healthy attitude.

Love,
Dad

Something to Think About:

1. There is always something someone can do better than you. What is your attitude about this?
2. Are you good at making others feel appreciated?
3. How often do you compliment someone else, especially someone in your family?

That Thing Called Work

Dear Jim,

The young people in our area are extremely fortunate. There are plenty of jobs for teenagers who want to work. Paper routes, lawn work, waiting on tables, and hospital jobs are just some. It's terrific for young people to have these opportunities.

In some areas of the nation jobs for teenagers are almost impossible to find. One large city has a 40% unemployment rate amoung young people.

There is no reason to overwork, but youth is a great time to learn some good work habits. If you start by learning to be a dependable employee, your skills will be well implemented.

It is like the Proverb that says, "A faithful employee is as refreshing as a cool day in the hot summertime" (25:13, TLB).

I have asked many employers what is the hardest part of their job. As I remember, all of them had the same answer. The help. Not the customer, or the product, or soaring interest rates, but people—those who work for them.

If there is one key to working well at a job, it must be the ability to get along with people. Those who quarrel, are jealous, or hot-headed make work difficult. Those who are pleasant and cooperative make things run more smoothly.

One employer said there is one skill young people are not learning. They are not learning to get along with others.

A second important thing to keep in mind is to be on time. Few faults are as aggravating as a late employee. Being late is a headache. Many good workers lose their jobs merely because they can't tell time.

A third guideline is to give your job your very best effort. Laziness is difficult to tolerate. Half a job will soon get you into trouble.

When I was in college I had a job for two weeks. I got

fired because I didn't have a good understanding of these three things. I spent the entire summer without a job and no money. It was a lesson well worth learning.

"A lazy fellow is a pain to his employers—like smoke in their eyes or vinegar that sets the teeth on edge" (Prov. 10:26, TLB).

Love,
Dad

Something to Think About:

1. What was your first job?
2. Name one person who is a good worker.
3. What are three keys to being a good worker.

Teenage Mothers

Dear Mary,

Every year thousands of nice, wholesome, kind teenage girls become pregnant. Some were sexually loose and didn't care. But most were filled with passion, felt loving, and didn't want to disappoint a guy.

Many teenage girls think they know all about pregnancy and don't want to discuss it. You are a knowledgeable, up-to-date young person. Just do yourself a favor, and look at some of these facts again.

Most teenage girls do not expect to get pregnant. It's one of those things that happens to others. Yet, one day they discover they are going to have a baby. They are going to be a mother. At that point their life begins to change rapidly.

Teenage pregnancy is so wide-spread in the United States that one out of ten girls is a mother before her eighteenth birthday. That means there are a large number of girls who are headed for unhappiness and disappointment.

It is often not only unhappy for themselves but frequently a very sad situation for the father of the child. A baby represents responsibility he probably is not ready to accept.

In many cases it is also tragic for the unborn baby. Half of the babies of these teenage mothers are presently aborted. Of those which are born, a far higher percentage are sick, handicapped, and underweight than those of older mothers. More of these babies die early and lower mental capacity is frequent.

There is more epilepsy, spinal injuries, head injuries, and limb defects. A child has a better chance if he is born to a mother in her twenties.

Even if a girl knows these facts, they probably won't mean much in a moment of passion when she is trying to decide whether or not to have sex. That's why it's important to rehearse them now, while you can listen carefully.

Why did God want us to wait until we were married before we had sex? Was He merely trying to hold back something good?

He understood that the secure, loving, committed way to enjoy each other was in marriage. Do yourself and everyone else a favor. Wait.

It's hard to wait. Sex sounds terrific—and it is. That's why it's worth waiting for.

"That is why I say to run from sex sin. No other sin affects your body as this one does" (1 Cor. 6:18, TLB).

Love,
Dad

Something to Think About:

1. What percentage of girls are mothers before their eighteenth birthday?
2. What disadvantages are there to becoming a mother before the age of twenty?
3. What percentage of babies of teenage mothers are aborted?

Teenage Fathers

Dear Jim,

One of your strong characteristics is taking responsibility. If we ask you to do something by a certain time, we can almost always count on it. That's a sign of maturity.

Don't grow up too fast. Enjoy being a happy teenager, but keep on acting in a mature, responsible way.

One of the big areas of responsibility is in your relationship to the opposite sex. A boy becomes involved with a girl, the girl becomes pregnant, and suddenly he is a father. Abruptly his days of youth and freedom are gone. Like lightening he must take on the full burden of being a parent.

A few boys don't care. They consider a pregnancy the girl's problem. Others, and I think you would be one, would accept his part of the responsibility.

It's tough being a teenage father. His life is turned upside down.

Generally he has to find work right away. That often means accepting a job without any training and pay that is usually peanuts.

Most boys have to receive financial help from their parents because they can't make it. That adds to the strain and the guilt he feels.

Usually his wife is unhappy. The suicide rate among teenage mothers is extremely high. Divorce among teenage marriages is enormous.

A father has legal responsibility for his child whether he marries the girl or not. Even 14-year-old fathers have been sued for financial support.

Many of these are just scare facts, but I think every teenage boy should know them. Teenage pregnancy is not merely a female problem. The father is also in for a long, tough road.

It's a big price to pay for a few minutes of sexual pleasure.

Some boys feel they have to have sex to prove they are men. Don't buy that junk. Sex never made anyone a man.

Others think they have to have sex because everyone is doing it. That's a bunch of garbage. Many young men, whom you respect, have decided to wait until they are married.

Being a teenage father is more trouble than it's worth.

"I would have you learn this great fact: that a life of doing right is the wisest life there is" (Prov. 5:11, TLB).

Love,
Dad

Something to Think About:

1. Are there teenage fathers in your community?
2. Is too much said about the teenage mother and too little about the teenage father?
3. Have you set some guidelines for the next few years of your life?

Religious Fog

Dear Mary,

It gets terribly confusing. There are all kinds of churches and denominations. How is anyone supposed to know what to believe or which to choose?

To make life more complicated, we are now invaded by every shade of cult, ism and sect. They are plucking people up like daisies.

How is a young person to know what to believe? Here are a few suggestions I hope will prove helpful.

First, and most important, put Jesus Christ as the object of your faith. We do not believe in a system, religion, or an organization. Our faith is in a person. That person is the only Son of God, Jesus Christ.

If everything else you believe crumbles, hold on to that central fact. When you invited Jesus Christ into your life, you found the essence of eternal life. Don't let anyone persuade you otherwise.

Peter said it best when Jesus asked him who he thought Jesus was. The fisherman answered:

"The Christ, the Messiah, the Son of the living God" (Matt. 16:16, TLB).

Second, be bold enough to read and interpret the Bible. If anyone claims you can't understand the Bible, become suspicious. Don't let anyone take your Bible away.

In most cults there is a strong leader who expects everyone to obey him. Don't fall for this mindless dribble. If they can stop you from thinking, they own you.

God has given us leaders and they can be of tremendous help. However, if anyone wants to do all your thinking and demands obedience, he is about as useful as a brick kite.

I met a girl who had fallen into the hands of a cult. At first they offered her great friendship and acceptance. She didn't have to think because they did it for her.

Soon she was completely cut off from her family. She

stopped taking care of herself. Since she was out of the habit of thinking, she could barely do it.

When people tried to rescue her from the cult, she didn't know whether to go or stay. She wasn't sure what was right or wrong.

Today this girl is free. She has found what she was really looking for. Jesus Christ has become part of her life.

It's easy to be sidetracked. It can be a miserable experience.

To know Jesus Christ is to be related to the living Son of God. It's the most important relationship.

Love,
Dad

Something to Think About:

1. Why do people follow cults?
2. Who is Jesus Christ?
3. What does Jesus Christ mean to you?

Parents Can Get Ridiculous

Dear June,

Do you ever think your parents make dumb rules? Do you ever wonder if they understand young people? Most teenagers begin to believe their parents are plainly ridiculous. They're often correct. Many times parents do make goofy decisions, and young people have to live with them.

A lot of teenagers know this, and so do many parents. If we had it to do over again, we would probably make a lot of decisions differently. Some rules would be easier—others would be more strict.

I have a feeling that ten years from now those rules won't make much difference. Was your bedtime fair? Why didn't we let you wear that dress or those jeans? Why did we make you clean the house, or why couldn't you sleep with the cat?

Thousands of decisions will be forgotten. But at the time they seemed right; we had your best interests at heart.

As you grow up I think only two questions will become all-important. The first one is, did we show you that we loved you? Most other things are passing and picky.

The question is not if we gave you everything you wanted. That isn't love. That's throwing out gifts without taking time to care. When we were stern, and when we were easy, the message had to be the same: We loved you.

That's the same message we receive from God. When we understand what He's doing, and when we don't understand, we still know He loves us.

The second question is, were we available? When someone had to make a decision *for* you, were we there? When someone had to make decisions *with* you, were we around? When you just needed to talk, were we there to listen? I hope so.

Love and availability.

Most of the time I think we made the right decisions. However, even when we were ridiculous, I hope these two messages stood out—love and availability.

"Children, obey your parents; this is the right thing to do because God has placed them in authority over you. Honor your father and mother. This is the first commandment that ends with a promise" (Eph. 6:1, TLB).

Love,
Dad

Something to Think About:

1. Are parents always right?
2. Should parents always be obeyed?
3. What two messages from your parents should reach you through your growing-up years?
4. Be open to discussion.

Dating with a Purpose

Dear Mary,

Sooner or later we all ask why. Why do men wear neck-ties? Why do we buy new clothes when the styles change? Why do we say "How are you?" when we really don't want an answer?

Life's little mysteries. They each deserve a healthy "Why?"

Dating is another puzzle. Fortunately it's a puzzle that has a solution. Why in the world do people bother to date?

There's more than one correct answer. There are also several lousy reasons to date. If you can sift them out in your own mind, I think your young years will run a great deal smoother.

First, a few lousy reasons to date. I think some girls date because they feel insecure. They are chasing love, and hope to find it by going out with guys.

This is a bummer. To them dating is not an interesting side of life. They see dating as the bread of life. It's date or die.

You don't have to roller skate or die. That would sound stupid. You don't have to play Monopoly or die. These are only parts of life. High-school dating is a small, nonessential sideline. Don't make it the main event.

You are complete. You are valuable. You are loved. You are needed. All of these are true even if you never date.

Another mistake is to date to build your reputation. Some young people are determined to become the envy of everyone. They date to find status. Sometimes they even date people with lousy character, or people with whom they have little in common, because to them dating is a chance to look like a big shot.

Being talked about isn't the thrill we might imagine. Trying to make others jealous is a worthless pastime. Being the conversation piece of gossip groups is as valuable as a hangnail.

Then what is the purpose of dating? Why are so many hypnotized by the subject?

In order for dating to be right, it has to have simple values. Dating has to have healthy, wholesome benefits. You can probably list a dozen good reasons to date. I'll settle for two—the two I think are the most important.

I'm reasonably sure Jesus Christ wasn't talking about dating when He said this. However, I am sure dating can be included in the statement:

Jesus said, "I am come that they might have life, and that they might have it more abundantly" (John 10:10, KJV).

He wants us to enjoy life. Life can be fun, exciting, interesting. That is what Christ wants for you.

I think the main purpose of dating is to have fun. For one evening enjoy a good time with one person. Don't raise the weighty questions of love, or attachment, or even, will he call again?

A date is one evening or afternoon where two people have a good time in each other's company. Keep it simple. Those who make it more than this end up with complications.

The second reason for dating is to get to know one person better. People are more fascinating than cars, new shoes, or social studies. You don't need to psychoanalyze each other. You don't need to come away with an in-depth character study. The evening will simply give you a better understanding of one person. To that extent your world is larger and fuller.

You can know someone better while skating, playing golf, eating pizza, or whatever.

If you keep a few healthy purposes in mind for dating, it leaves a pleasant taste. If you fix on some lousy purposes, dating can become sour.

Thanks for thinking it through.

Love,
Dad

Something to Think About:

1. What do you think is the main purpose of dating at your age?
2. What are some of the benefits of dating?
3. Is dating absolutely essential to life?

Looking through the Fence

Dear Jim,

Never be content to go through life looking through the fence. At practically any ball game you can see young people standing around watching the game, but never playing.

Most likely they would love to be inside on a team, giving it their all. They are often eating their heart out watching someone else participate.

Don't settle for it, Jim. Don't be content to watch life go by. Join the teams, find out what you enjoy, and jump in.

Young people can also be found standing around at play rehearsals. They wish they had the nerve to try out, but instead they shrink back and let others do it.

The same is true about classroom participation. Some speak out while others only wish they could.

I dare you, Jim, to pick out what you really like to do and jump into the middle. Give it a try.

All of us have a few talents that will starve to death. We have never recognized them, fed them, and allowed them to grow.

Have you ever heard someone say he didn't like chess, and then you found he has never played it? Some people do not like golf because they spent one afternoon playing it and couldn't unlock the game's mysteries.

If we lock the doors, it is a little harder to unlock them later. Once we have said "I can't" to something, it is difficult to get up enough nerve to try it later.

We don't have to try everything. Not everything is suited to our abilities and interests. However, it would really be foolish to let life glide past because we weren't daring enough to give it a try.

You know you have God-given talents. That's a great feeling. Every person is gifted. Some wait longer to find out what their gifts are. Unfortunately, a few will *never* know what they are.

It would be easy to list ten things you do well. I dare you to find out if there are more. The best way to find out is by trying, and trying, and trying again.

Reach out and enjoy the excellent abilities God has given you. It would be silly for any of us to go through life just looking through the fence.

"Being confident of this very thing, that he who hath begun a good work in you will perform it until the day of Jesus Christ" (Phil. 1:6, KJV).

Love,
Dad

Something to Think About:

1. Are you too involved in activities or sports? Not involved enough?
2. What is your favorite activity? What do you enjoy most?
3. Try something new. You may surprise yourself.

It's Hard to Stop

Dear Jim,

We don't decide to begin a bad habit. People don't usually wake up one morning and say, "I think I'll begin a lousy habit today. I'll start chewing socks."

Habits normally creep up on us. Just like good habits, they gradually become part of our life. When habits become routine, they are difficult to change.

You are doing a good job of cultivating healthy habits. You save money like a bear watching her cubs. When it comes to keeping your word no one does a better job. You even brush your teeth as though your life depended on it. All of these are strong foundation blocks for building a good future.

As you develop good habits, make sure the bad ones don't creep up on you. Don't play with anything that could be addictive. And that means *anything*.

Someone said a child smokes to prove he is a man. Twenty years later he tries to stop smoking to prove the same thing.

Smoking is a bummer. So is alcohol abuse. Every young person should know what miserable slave drivers these habits are. Once they grab hold of your body, they don't let go easily.

You know that. So do most teenagers. The mystery is why so many allow themselves to become addicted. The numbers still continue to grow.

Eating the wrong things can also become a habit. For years we train ourselves to eat all kinds of junk. Later our bodies rebel against it and we pay a price. Don't develop the habit of living off pop and chips. It could be hard to switch to real food.

Habit isn't a dirty word. Good study habits mold our lives. Many intelligent students do poorly in school simply because of poor study habits. With a little effort we can develop good habits.

It's hard to plan for tomorrow. Most young people have the great gift of living one day at a time. However, tomorrow cannot be ignored. The habits we develop as young people play a big factor in what our future will be like.

Bad habits are like picking up huge stones. They slow us down. They make slaves of us. They become burdens we don't really need.

A wise person cultivates good habits.

"Have two goals: wisdom—that is, knowing and doing right—and common sense. Don't let them slip away, for they fill you with living energy, and are a feather in your cap" (Prov. 3:21, 22, TLB).

Love,
Dad

Something to Think About:

1. Name five good habits you have.
2. Name one habit you would like to change.
3. Think of ways you can change that habit.

Double-Dating

Dear Mary,

That sounds great! Four people having a great time together for the evening is really first class. Especially when you don't know your date very well, another couple helps you to relax. You can bounce your conversation off three other people and often the whole evening is more fun.

If you want to suggest a double date, make sure it doesn't come across too forcefully. You don't want to make the guy feel that you are afraid of him. Suggest double-dating in such a way that he will feel free to turn it down if he wants to.

Naturally, it's better if he knows the other couple. There's no sense in making him feel like an outsider on his own date.

I double-dated several times and learned some things I wish I had known beforehand. I'll throw them out. They may be of some help to you before you jump in.

One thing to keep in mind is to find a couple who is on the same level of relationship that you and your date are. My girl and I dated with a couple who were engaged. It presented some tense moments. We barely knew each other, and the engaged couple couldn't leave each other alone! They were kissing in the restaurant and on the golf course. We wanted to run away and hide from embarrassment.

There can be a lot of pressure to do things you don't want to do or aren't ready for. Casual daters are better off with casual daters.

Another area to consider is where you are going and what you are going to do. If the other couple has widely different taste than yours, you could wind up doing something you and your date don't enjoy at all.

On the whole, though, double-dating has some real advantages. Have fun!

Love,
Dad

Something to Think About:

1. Have you ever double-dated? How did it go?
2. What are some advantages of double-dating?
3. What are some considerations before planning a double date?

Date and Tell?

Dear Mary,

It's only normal to talk about your date. Whom did you go out with? Where did you go? Did you have fun? We all like to talk about things that are important to us.

However, there should be some boundaries on what we say. A person has spent the evening with you. That person is often unsure and nervous. Often he either says or does something that's really dumb. Do your friend a favor and don't tell everything to your other friends.

Maybe your date said something that shocked you. Possibly it was a far-out political view, maybe it was some trouble he has with a personal habit. Either way there is something sacred about your conversation.

It's tacky to hurt the reputation of someone who spent an evening sharing with you.

That doesn't mean a date has to be a secret, hush-hush operation. There are so many good, fun things to tell your friends. But remember, conversation has boundaries. Only fools cross them.

Maybe your date has a moral standard which is lower than yours. That's always awkward. But that's still no reason to smear his reputation. Your date is maturing and growing. Keep your standard firm as stone. However, don't run him down to your friends.

You may later find that he has tremendous respect for your standard. Your firmness (and quietness) may be a gigantic help to him.

There are two sides to this coin. When you go out on a date, everything you say and do may be front-page news in school tomorrow.

We used to say that boys always kiss and tell. That's still true today. Some very naive young lady may think that what they did on a date was just between the two of them. The next day she discovers their date is a public bulletin.

Doubtless some of these stories are flat lies. Some guys try to inflate their own egos this way.

It's fun to share, but make sure you do it with someone you trust.

There is only one person you can control. Yourself! Do it, and you will feel good about yourself and you will be well thought of.

"A wise man holds his tongue. Only a fool blurts out everything he knows: that only leads to sorrow and trouble" (Prov. 10:14, TLB).

Love,
Dad

Something to Think About:

1. Do you know someone who can't keep a secret?
2. Have you ever had someone tell a secret you trusted them with? How did it feel?
3. To keep something to yourself you know has been told in confidence is a sign of maturity.

Clear the Road!

Dear Jim,

It will be great when you can drive. You show a steady maturity and I know you will take the responsibility seriously. (Besides, it will be good when you can take your sister to piano lessons.)

But before you take over the wheel and push the steel monster down the highway, there are a few suggestions I'd like to throw in.

Teenage boys have a reputation for driving like maniacs. And this isn't a rumor. No one is picking on the youth of our country, but some teenage boys drive like the whole world is a demolition derby. (Some girls could be included here.)

This isn't necessary. Teenagers can be great drivers. You can be one, too.

Prove you're ready to drive by showing a steady hand. Don't fall into the trap of driving "crazy" to prove you are daring. I had a teenage friend who did that. If he hadn't been showing off, he would be 42 now.

So many young people seem to enjoy throwing gravel, driving on lawns and passing everybody on the road. It's hard to resist temptation. There is always pressure from others to drive like a fool.

But you *can* drive like a responsible person. I know you can do it, because you are responsible in other areas. Thanks for not being a stunt man on the road.

Another guideline to remember is don't play games with the police. They aren't the bad guys. They are there for your protection.

Too many young people, and adults as well, take the attitude of "let's outsmart the cops." It's a dumb attitude. Forget it.

A CB radio can be fun. But if its used to locate the police and speed when they aren't around, it's a mistake.

Some young people have seen adults breaking the law and then bragging about it. It's like receiving adult approval for speeding. This is unfortunate.

The entire matter breaks down to respect for other people. If we drive carelessly, we're taking the chance of injuring someone else. We can't take that chance.

You aren't empty-headed. There is no need to prove you can be daring. Show respect for people and their property, and have many happy years behind the wheel.

Love,
Dad

Something to Think About:

1. Do you think young people are good drivers or poor drivers? Explain.
2. Why do some people drive foolishly?
3. Do adults set bad examples?
4. What is the real reason for driving carefully?

Just Look at Yourself

Dear Mary,

John was a boring kid. Not many people are really boring, but John won the prize. He managed to wrap practically every conversation around himself. Like fish left in the hot sun, he began to stink.

We all know someone like this. The conversation can start on any subject—baseball, cyclones or nuclear physics. No matter where it begins, everyone knows where it will end—on John.

It's tough when you see yourself as the center of the universe. Then flowers, cars, mountains, orphans, robots, or whatever, only have meaning to the extent that they affect you. No topic of conversation is interesting to the self-centered person unless he can somehow bring it back it himself.

I'm glad you are not like John. You are important, significant, even fascinating, but hardly the center of the universe.

All of us should take a careful look at who we are. Some calm reflection and soul-searching evaluation is tremendous. But too much internalizing may turn us into self-centered, overstuffed bores.

It's helpful to look at ourselves. We mature by applying the Scriptures to our lives, and grow because of it. We cleanse ourselves by letting the Word of God search us out. If we do it regularly, we can build a strong inner stability.

However, don't let it turn to self-centeredness.

That's part of the reason why it's important to support a Laotian family. It gets our eyes off ourselves. That's why you need to help an elderly family move. That's why you collect winter coats for poor children. Self-centeredness only rots and ruins. Caring and sharing is a healthy practice.

Paul's words keep us in balance. "Don't think about

your own affairs, but be interested in others, too, and in what they are doing" (Phil. 2:4, TLB).

There are people all around you who need you. Some are lonely and afraid. A few feel rejected and don't think they fit in. Once in a while a friend has trouble at home. You aren't a pastor or a professional counselor, but you are a friend and a Christian.

Our problems seem smaller when we reach out to someone else in need.

Love,
Dad

Something to Think About:

1. Name three things you do for your own good.
2. Name three things you do for others.
3. Why is it good to help others?

Prejudice

Dear June,

Many of us grew up disliking, distrusting and even hating people of other races and cultures. We often thought that if someone was not the same color as us, he had to be inferior in some way.

I think you are growing up in a more understanding, tolerant world. I hope you will never dislike someone because of the color of his skin.

Your involvement with our Laotian family might help a great deal. We see them caring, feeling, hurting, working, loving, and we can see how much we are alike. Their customs and habits may be different from ours, but that doesn't make either one of us inferior—only different.

A healthy love in Christ can go a long way in helping us love each other. It can tear down walls and prejudices and teach us to accept one another.

Paul put it this way, "We are no longer Jews or Greeks or slaves or free men or even merely men or women, but we are all the same—we are Christians; we are one in Christ Jesus" (Gal. 3:23, TLB).

Let your friendships cross racial and national lines. Your life will grow by hearing the rich experiences others have had.

A great deal of prejudice still exists. If this doesn't ease, many people will suffer. It's important for Christians to reach out and show that love in Christ cannot be shackled by racial differences.

When I began high school, the races were separated and there were only white students in our school. When blacks and whites integrated, many people became upset. However, when the noise calmed down we were surprised to see how well we got along.

Soon some of my best friends were people of other races—Fan, from China, and Lawrence, the black president of our senior class. They were terrific human beings. It didn't take long to become good friends with good people.

Keep your life open. Some of the really great poeple you will get to know will come from other races and cultures.

Love,
Dad

Something to Think About:

1. Do you have friends among other races? Name some things that you have learned through these friendships.
2. Would you like to spend a summer in another country? Where? Why?
3. Does color or culture make a person inferior or superior?

Down-in-the-Mouth

Dear Mary,

We will never know how talented Chuck was. There were so many things he could do. Everyone believed he had ability—that is, everyone except Chuck.

Instead of accepting the fact that he had gifts, Chuck was busy denying it. If someone said he played ball well, he would spend the next few minutes denying it. He had a terminal case of the "can'ts." No amount of facts, encouragement, or insults could convince him otherwise.

Chuck had flunked in attitude and he refused to turn it around.

Before Chuck tried anything, he already knew exactly how it would come out. He was going to lose. He was so persuaded that he would fall on his face that he almost always did.

In our family we can often see this problem in each other. Sometimes we turn shy and put ourselves down. We look at opportunities as huge, insurmountable difficulties.

Down-in-the-mouth is what we used to call it. It's a put-down of ourselves. It's a pity party. Poor me, I can't do anything right.

Thinking we will fail becomes a habit. I think you are only now beginning to realize what you can do. That's great. It's a healthy attitude.

Your future is bright. You have much to give and much to enjoy. Don't trade that colorful tomorrow for a dull bowl of the "I can'ts."

Every Christian has good reason to be an optimist. Your future is as full and as fascinating as Jesus Christ himself. You are a winner if you see yourself that way. Each individual is a winner in Jesus Christ if he will allow himself to be.

Every time you hear yourself putting yourself down, remember that you are making a choice. It would be just as easy to say "I can," "I will", and grab life by the horns.

"So don't be anxious about tomorrow. God will take care of your tomorrow, too. Live one day at a time" (Matt. 6:34, TLB).

Love,
Dad

Something to Think About:

1. Why should every Christian be an optimist?
2. Do you put yourself down?
3. How can you encourage someone who doesn't use his full potential?

Running Away

Dear Jim,

Don't be surprised if sometime you feel like running away from home. Most young people probably think about it sooner or later. Even some adults want to get away from it all.

Three-quarters of a million young people under the age of 18 run away each year. That's a great number of families that are upset, shocked, and hurt because someone has disappeared. Many runaways only spend one night away from home. Others are never seen or heard from again.

It might be hard to believe, but one runaway out of five may have been fairly happy at home. Twenty percent run away purely for the adventure of it. They want to see what California looks like, or check out the Rocky Mountains.

Your grandfather Coleman did just that. He joined the Navy when he was just a teenager. But, his mother had him sent home.

Most runaway adventures cause a tremendous amount of heartache. The parents are worried sick. Unfortunately, some end up hurt, in trouble with the law, or worse.

A small number of runaways are actually pushed out of their homes. Their parents feel they can no longer handle them or simply don't want them around.

The great majority of runaways are those who weren't getting along with people. They thought their parents were mean, laid down too many laws, or just didn't care about them.

Others were having friction with teachers, schoolmates, or brothers and sisters.

It's easy to understand why people want to run away. Sometimes the pressures of life become too great. Sometimes we wonder if anyone understands. Every now and again we wonder if anybody even cares.

Many young people probably run away for a day, maybe

just an afternoon. They are frustrated, and don't know what to do. I wouldn't be surprised if you have run away—if just for a few hours.

Pressure seems to build up when a young person and a parent don't understand each other. That's why talking is so important. The young person needs to explain exactly how he feels. It might not change the parent's mind, but at least the parent will come closer to understanding. And miraculously, parents sometimes do change their minds.

It's also important for the young person to hear how the parent feels. Often children don't really understand where their parents are coming from.

Talking might not change the rule or get you out of a job; however, talking will reduce the friction and increase the understanding. And sometimes it even changes a rule.

"Listen to your father's advice and don't despise an old mother's experiences. Get the facts at any price, and hold on tightly to all the good sense you can get" (Prov. 23:22, 23, TLB).

Love,
Dad

Something to Think About:

1. What are some good ways to let off pressure?
2. What are some guidelines to help keep pressure from building up?
3. Do you have friends who have run away from home? Explain.

Parking

Dear Mary,

Whenever I get a chance to sing my one-note song, I do it. And every time I hear young people snicker, and say it's silly. Undaunted and stubborn, here I go again: *Don't sit in a parked car!*

It's convenient and cozy, and so relaxing to sit with a friend in the car after a date and merely talk. If you care for each other much at all, you are probably playing with fire.

There, I said it again. Go ahead and chuckle. Who wants to listen to a parent with gray temples and an old green Dodge?

But, the facts remain the same. It's too easy to become cuddly and soon become more sexually involved than you want to. Heads quickly surrender to hearts and before long passion becomes the champion.

Well-meaning young people easily compromise more than they ever intended. It's natural. It's normal. It's even healthy. But, the timing is off. It is a sexual involvement that neither person is ready for.

The minute you park the car, be smart, and get right out. If you're at home, or on the date, or just stopping to talk, talk outside the car.

It isn't because boys are big bad monsters trying to lead little girls astray. But because both of you are human and aware of the temptations involved.

Dating doesn't need to involve a crazy fear of sex. Millions of boys and girls go out, have a good time, and never become physically involved. However, it still makes sense to take reasonable precautions for the sake of both of you.

It may sound too simple, almost comical, to get this kind of advice. However, I think it is among the most practical you can get.

Thanks for listening, Mary, (You can go ahead and laugh out loud now.)

"Flee fornication" (1 Cor. 6:18, KJV).

Love,
Dad

Something to Think About:

1. Name five good things to do on a date.
2. Why is talking in a parked car not a good idea?
3. What are some alternatives?

How to Say No

Dear Mary,

Something is wacky. I'm not sure what it is, so obviously I don't know how to solve it. We have young people, years away from marriage, who are dying for sex. Is this because our society has put too much emphasis on sex? Or is it because we have been too secretive about it? Or is it because youth are waiting too long to get married?

If I solve that one, I should win the Nobel Peace Prize.

However we got here, the fact is that many people are tremendously turned on. Not everyone, but many. This complicates dating. Instead of the date being a social outlet and learning situation, too often it turns into a mating call. Dating doesn't have to be a sexual escapade. It won't be if you can keep your cool.

Sometime you might meet a boy who is part octopus. He is all arms and hands, When you do, you will have to establish the rules. He won't have enough sense to.

If his hands are determined to roam around, you will have to say no. His mind is made up about what he wants to do; now he needs to hear from you.

The most obvious thing you can do is to say "no." That sounds simple, and probably will work. However, I have now learned there is more than one way of saying "no." The way you say it will determine what happens to your relationship.

First, you can say "no" and mean "maybe." Your tone of voice and your actions are more convincing than your words. While your word draws a line, your voice says you aren't sure.

Establish your standard now. Dating doesn't have to be a wrestling match. First, be convinced that you need to set the standard with conviction. A weak "no" is worthless.

A second kind of "no" is cold, harsh and ugly. It sounds like "Go eat worms." It makes your date feel rejected as a person, and often it ends your friendship.

A third way to say "no" is the better idea. It is firm, but caring. You could say, "I like you too much to do that," and pull away. Or else, "I want to be friends, but we can't be that way."

Then, immediately make a suggestion: "Let's go get a Coke," or, "Call me tomorrow." Aim to remove some of the embarrassment. Help the guy out of the fix he has gotten himself into. That makes you a real friend.

Some boys are not as mature as girls. They may not have as good a concept of boundaries as you do. If you say "no" in a caring way, you may be able to keep a friend. You will be doing him a huge favor.

But what if he persists? What if the caring "no" doesn't work? Then tell him to go eat worms.

Love,
Dad

Something to Think About:

1. Do you find it hard to say "no" in any circumstance (even when people ask you to do favors you can't)?
2. What is the best way to be a friend to a date who can't keep his or her hands to himself?
3. Would you go out again with someone who is an octopus?
4. Does a date have to be a physical encounter to be a success?

You Were Absolutely Right

Dear Jim,

Sometimes adults get down on young people and talk like they can't do anything right. It must be a terrible feeling. You need to know that so often you *have* been right and adults have been wrong.

Do you remember the day the police called? (It really rattles a parent when the police call!) They wanted to know if you had broken the pipes on the construction site.

They checked your tennis shoes for signs of cement. They wanted to know where you were at a certain time. From their questions, they seemed to assume you were guilty.

Thanks for being cool. You answered their questions straightforwardly. You were polite and clear-headed. There was no belligerence, only respect.

Inside, you knew you were innocent. It was tough for a while, but you held firm. I remember how relieved I was a few days later when the chief said, "Don't worry about Jim. He didn't have anything to do with it."

You were right.

There were also times when you were dead wrong. Unfortunately, those are the times you hear about the most.

Sometimes adults have owed you an apology. It isn't easy for parents to apologize. It wrecks our self-image. We like to think we're all-wise, filled with experience and bubbling over with knowledge. That's why it hurts to say, "I'm sorry, I was wrong."

When a parent apologizes, he does something special. He says he was wrong and his child was right. You ought to write those times down. They don't come often.

Feel good about yourself. You aren't wrong just because

you are young. But when you are wrong, don't be afraid to admit it.

Love,
Dad

Something to Think About:

1. Do you think adults usually trust or distrust young people? Explain.
2. If you are wrongly accused, how should you react?
3. Why is it hard to apologize?
4. When did you last tell your parents you were sorry? When did they last apologize to you?

Enjoying a Full Life

Dear June,

Do you know anyone who is overloaded in one direction? Maybe his entire life is given over to sports, or he reads most of the time. It's hard to get the most out of life when everything centers on one activity.

Sports fanatics often get lopsided. Everything depends on what the team does. If the White Sox lose a game, the rest of their day is shot. If Pittsburgh loses its quarterback, they get down in the dumps.

The person who has many interests avoids these emotional dungeons. If one thing doesn't go well, the well-rounded person bounces back. His happiness doesn't depend on a single event.

That's why I feel sorry for the girl who is "boy-crazy." Her every day seems to hang on one thin thread. If she is getting along great with the boys, she is riding high. When they give her the cold shoulder, she heads right for the pits.

This type of girl doesn't control her own life. Someone else decides what kind of day she will have. If a boy smiles, she is set free to enjoy herself. When the boys avoid her or frown, she becomes a slave to gloom.

All of us suffer from this to some degree. We want people to like us and give their approval. The problem comes when we take it too seriously.

I once knew a girl who had one goal in life: she wanted boys to like her. When they cared, she felt worthwhile and valuable. Consequently, she did some terribly foolish things. She had to do them, because to her, boys were all that made life meaningful.

Keep your interests as wide and varied as they are. When your softball team loses, you practice your flute. When you can't find anyone to go bowling with, you read a book or bake cookies. When your "favorite" boy ignores you, you find a girlfriend and play tennis.

God didn't create a one-dimensional world. When one thing goes flat, there are plenty of other facinating things to do.

Paul understood the well-balanced life. When things were going well, he was satisfied. If something turned sour, he was still stable as a rock.

"Not that I speak in respect of want: for I have learned, in whatsoever state I am, therewith to be content" (Phil. 4:11, KJV).

Try not to be a victim. Don't let what others say and do control your life. God gave us too rich a world to waste moping over some little event. Keep your life active, interesting, and productive.

You're off to a great start. Your interests are wide and your life is full. The teen years should be among your happiest years.

Love,
Dad

Something to Think About:

1. What are five of your chief interests?
2. How do you stop from being "boy-crazy?"
3. What new thing would you like to try?
4. Why is it important to have more than one interest?

Are Boys Better?

Dear Mary,

It is deeply woven into our thinking. We often feel that girls are nice, but boys are better. That mentality may be dying in our society, but it doesn't give up easily. There are some statistics which claim that most families want a boy. A girl is all right, but the parents' heart is set on a male.

This is just another way that you and your sister have helped me. You have opened my eyes to the great fun there is in having girls in the family. You are exciting, helpful, intelligent—in every way an equal to your brother. I hope many of the present prejudices against girls will be forgotten by the time you have children.

Things have improved for women. A hundred years ago it was nearly impossible for a girl to get into medical school. Today the freshman class in a medical school near here is fifty percent women. Women now graduate from service academies, head businesses, and fill other professional roles.

Not long ago, a boy and a girl both scored equally well on their academic tests. The teacher could not praise the boy enough, but the girl was ignored. Was it because the teacher didn't think the girl could advance with her high academic potential?

Jesus didn't hold prejudices against women. He included people like Mary Magdalene into the very heart of His ministry. Jesus stopped to speak to the woman at the well regardless of what others might have thought.

The Son of God was and is a friend of women.

If you want to see the high regard we should have for females, read Proverbs 31. The good woman was one who had the freedom to go out into the community and fully participate.

She could look over a field and buy it. She could conduct

a business. She could oversee her household and employees.

That doesn't mean you have to copy the woman in Proverbs 31. However, it does mean the biblical concept of womanhood offers you fantastic freedom. Sometimes, more freedom than our society is willing to admit.

At the last check a woman made 59¢ for each dollar a man made for doing the same job. That's unfair. It's prejudice.

God loves women and men and He loves us equally.

Love,
Dad

Something to Think About:

1. Are girls and boys treated equally in the athletic program at your school? Explain.
2. Are more boys than girls elected to offices in your school?
3. Are women and men treated equally in your community? Name some examples.
4. Does God consider men and women equal?

Getting Even

Dear Jim,

I just finished a fantasic family seminar in Lincoln, and there is one thing I particularly want to pass on. It's really worth remembering.

One of the speakers was the famous Dr. Karl Menninger. At 87 years of age, many believe he is the greatest living psychiatrist.

Dr. Menninger asked the hundreds of delegates what was the worst disease in the world. Sociologists, psychologists, and social workers all scratched their heads. Then the wise doctor gave his answer: Revenge. People feel they have to get even with someone.

Not afraid to quote from the Bible, Dr. Menninger reminded us that vengeance belongs to God. But, he said, we don't trust God, so we decide to take care of it ourselves.

Revenge causes tension. Every time someone insults us it makes us want to snap back at them. When a car cuts in front of us on the highway, we often want to tear ahead and "teach them a lesson."

Only God knows how many people are dead because of vengeance. How many countries have gone to war? How many homes have been set afire? How many have been shot or stabbed because someone had to get even?

Over and over again you will feel the need to hurt someone. You will want to punch him, break something, really tell him off. Treat that temptation like a grizzly bear. Once you let it loose there is no telling what havoc it might raise.

There are too many people in prison merely because they wanted a few minutes of revenge. Now they have years to sit behind stone walls and think about what they have done.

A fire chief was asked why there was so much arson. His reply was short and direct, "Revenge." People go out of their minds trying to get even.

Getting even is not a sign of manhood. Letting your passions go wild is not macho. Self-control, forgiveness, patience, understanding—these are the solid qualities of a real man.

You need to let a lot go by. Don't jump whenever something happens that you don't like.

If God wants to exercise His vengeance, leave it up to Him. He doesn't need our help.

Love,
Dad

Something to Think About:

1. Can you give instances where revenge was the cause of injury or destruction of property?
2. What do you do when someone treats you wrongly?
3. Can you think of instances where Christ was treated wrongly? What did He do?

Going Steady

Dear Mary,

There are so many beautiful things about going steady. Sometimes we adults forget how good it was, or could be.

What am I talking about? When I say going steady, I mean dating only one person, constantly. Going *steadily*— dating one person often but also being open to date others—is another matter.

When you go with one person for a long time, you really get to know him well. You have someone who cares. He knows what your favorite color is, what your dreams for to-morrow are, and what gripes you most. That can't be all bad.

If you break your arm, he might send you a card, or maybe even a rose. Sometimes, you might wear his class ring.

When you are really down or disgusted, you have some-one to talk to about it. And it is a little neater just because he is of the opposite sex.

Having someone who cares about you all the time makes you feel special. It adds a certain amount of stability to your life.

Going steady has more benefits than a union contract.

But—for all of its beauty and strength, I also see going steady as a loser. On the bottom line, it can be a bummer.

Your friends probably won't agree with me. You might not either. But from what I have seen and what I have done, I detect some heavy drawbacks.

To begin with, going steady is more of an involvement than two high-school students are generally prepared to make. Your future is in a fog. As you continue to grow, your values and goals will change. You're in a shifting trend, and it is too soon to tie yourself to one person.

Going steady could be a deeper commitment than you need right now.

I don't doubt that two young people can love each other. However, it is usually a frustrating, unbalanced love, because it can't be consummated. It is like buying a box of candy that you can't eat for four years.

You would be far better off to wait awhile before buying the candy. Your taste in sweets may change!

I think the physical temptation for sexual satisfaction is greater if you are going steady. This isn't always the case, just 99 times out of 100.

Continued close contact results in familiarity. Familiarity blossoms into adventure. Adventure gives birth to conquest. Going steady is playing with sexual fire. Not everyone gets burned, but too many do.

If someone is already going steady, he usually doesn't care to listen. He's convinced he has found four acres of heaven! But since you aren't going steady, I'll throw in my two cents.

Learn to know several guys on a friendly basis. They can help you to understand humanity. There will be plenty of time for a deep commitment later.

I went steady for two years. (It's probably hard for you to imagine an old geezer like me going steady.) It was so nice, and she was terrific! But if I had it to do over again, I wouldn't.

Wait until later for the deep commitment. You will be able to handle it a lot better.

Love,
Dad

Something to Think About:

1. What do you think of going steady?
2. What is your opinion of some friends who go steady? Are they having a good time? Are they becoming more involved than they would like?
3. What are some of the problems with going steady?
4. What are some of the advantages of *not* going steady?

Carry a Quarter

Dear June,

Linda discovered she was in the wrong car and wanted out. It had sounded like fun at first. Some boys she barely knew asked Linda and her girlfriend to jump in and go along for a Coke. Without thinking, the two girls piled in.

The car had not gone far before Linda grew tense. The boys' language was a lot rougher than she was used to. Their idea of a joke wasn't the same as hers. Suddenly it occurred to her that she wasn't even sure where they were going.

Finally, Linda said she wanted out. She didn't want to be a drag or sound dumb, but she also didn't like the way it was coming together. So they stopped the car, and she got out.

Do yourself a favor, and always carry a quarter! If things start to go in a direction that makes you nervous, give me a call. Wherever you are and whatever hour it is I will come and get you. Your quarter is your insurance policy. When you need out, you can be sure of an exit.

This isn't an attempt to scare you. You probably will never have to do this. Most people don't. However, if things get tense, for whatever reason, you will know exactly what to do.

Even good, dependable friends can sometimes do weird things. Someone decides to try racing his car. Another person wants to see what it's like to drink. The group gets a brainstorm to go someplace where they don't belong.

Normally people think clearly, but once in a while we all get flaky ideas. That might be the time to say calmly, "I think I'll just go home." You aren't making a big scene or trying to prove you are better. You merely know where the danger line is and decide not to cross it.

When I read about a carload of kids who were killed, I wondered about the riders. Did all of them approve of the speeding? Did anyone object? Did anybody ask to get out?

It is too late to ask them now, but maybe it could have been different for some of them.

Carry a quarter. You will probably never need it. You have a terrific group of friends. But if you ever do need a ride home, just give me a call.

Love,
Dad

Something to Think About:

1. Have you ever felt you were about to get into trouble? Explain, if you can.
2. What did you do about it?
3. Do you think it's worth "losing face" to back out of a tight spot?

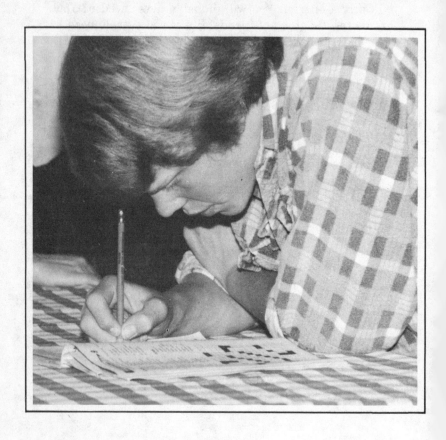

The New Kid in Town

Dear Mary,

When automobiles were first manufactured in the United States, the idea caught on slowly. People were in no hurry to give up their horses. After all, how could they know the automobile would last? There was a real problem with the tires, especially on poor roads where nails and other debris were scattered.

People waited awhile to see if the automobile would prove itself.

That may be good advice when it comes to a watch or video game. But it's poor advice when it comes to people.

Too often we sit back and cautiously eye the new person in town. We want to wait and see what he is like before we get too close. It might take us six months of careful scrutiny before we decide it is safe to befriend him.

This isn't only a trait of young people. Adults, too, often stand off, suspiciously, afraid to get involved too quickly.

It might help us to be more outgoing if we would remember what it felt like for *us* to be the new kid in town. The new kid in school. The new kid in church. The new kid in the neighborhood.

Most of us felt nervous, uncertain, waiting to see if we would be accepted. Sometimes the first few weeks or months can be very rough.

This is one more place where I think Christians should be different. We should be caring, loving, and sensitive to people's feelings. We should reach out, and reach out soon!

But there is a risk in reaching out. We may wonder if we are going to be rejected or get involved with someone we really won't like. Christians should get used to taking risks. We know that most people will accept an honest offer of friendship.

A dad once told me, "My daughter didn't have any trouble moving into this town. The young people just seemed to include her and accept her right away."

Fantastic! It would be great if every young person could be welcomed that warmly. They should be strangers only briefly.

Jesus taught us a strange thing. He said that when we befriend the new kid, we are really being a friend to Him.

"For I was hungry and you fed me; I was thirsty and you gave me water; I was a stranger and you invited me into your homes" (Matt.25:35, TLB).

It's an important part of life. There is no fun in being left out or ignored. By getting to know the new kid, we not only make his life better, but we add to our own.

I think you do it well, Mary. Never give up the art.

Love,
Dad

Something to Think About:

1. Do you recall being a newcomer?
2. How did you feel?
3. What are some things you could do to make a new person feel welcome?

Someone to Talk To

Dear Jim,

Whom do you like to talk to? Whom do you like to bounce ideas off to get his opinion? It sounds simple, but having someone to talk to is a big part of life.

There was once a girl who needed someone to talk to. She had some personal problems and needed to express them. So, she went to a young adult counselor and found some solid help.

Unfortunately, her parents were furious. They didn't want someone else helping their child. Before long, they made a nasty scene.

I'm glad you have people to talk to. We all need someone. You have your parents, but naturally we have our limitations. Friends are great, and I suspect you share lots of ideas with them. Your older sister likes to share thoughts with you.

When something is bugging you, I hope you will find someone to unload on. If you feel you need to reach out to a new person, I hope you will do it.

I've met many young people who have felt terribly confused. Some saw life as too heavy a burden. They wanted to talk to someone, but never found the freedom. Eventually, they did some sad things to themselves, partly because they kept their problems inside instead of talking them out with someone.

A wise man wrote: "Plans go wrong with too few counselors; many counselors bring success" (Prov. 15:22, TLB).

There are a number of good, understanding people around.

Pastor Olson is a level-headed guy. You could give him a call and ask him about most anything. He has helped me many times.

Dr. Wilcox is another who understands young people, and you can tell he really likes them.

Your school counselors seem like excellent people. Don't be afraid to drop in on them.

Your mom and dad want to listen, discuss, and help if we can. But, in some cases, it might not be possible. We'd rather you talked it over with someone else than let it burn inside.

There are a few young people who get into trouble partly because they have no one to talk to. More than one person has dropped out of school because he didn't feel free to talk. Some regrets might have been avoided if the young person could have found a friendly ear.

It's good to share ideas with you. But when you need another listener, I hope you will feel free to find a good one.

Love,
Dad

Something to Think About:

1. Whom do you find it easy to share with?
2. If you had a serious problem, whom might you go to?
3. Why is it important not to keep problems bottled up inside?

A Different Kind of Love

Dear Mary,

The subject has become so common now that it has almost turned comical. A leading tennis star recently admitted that she had had a homosexual affair. The nation was shocked, and soon turned to a flood of new jokes.

She is far from the only one. Political figures, football players, and thousands of others have announced that they have had affairs. Many discuss it on television.

Recently, a gay chorus was scheduled to sing in a church in Lincoln and appear on television. A huge roar of protest erupted and the TV appearance was cancelled.

It looks as if you will live in a society which has many open homosexuals. The word isn't whispered anymore. You will probably know one or more people who are homosexual, if you do not already.

Let me offer some suggestions that might come in handy. There is no reason to over-react to the subject.

Homosexuals are people—do not hate them. When you hear of someone beating up a homosexual, you wonder who has the worse problem. Jesus loved adulterers. I believe He would have had no trouble loving homosexuals.

Jesus loves me. That is proof that He can love anyone. Never hate someone because he is different or wrong.

Remember that almost all, if not all, homosexuals choose to live that way. God did not create them as homosexuals. God loves them, but He is not responsible for their choice.

They have found it easier to relate to and love someone of their own sex. It is a people problem.

It can be very difficult to get along with people. After a few bad experiences and rejections, I can understand why someone may be attracted to a friend of his/her own sex. But, that doesn't make it right. I understand why some people steal and why others lie. But, they aren't right either. Sin is still sin.

If we hate homosexuals, *we* are wrong. When we are their friend and try to help them, our actions are as they should be as Christians.

It would be easy to hate the tennis player who told the world she had a homosexual affair. That would be the natural reaction for many. It is something else to reach out, understand, and try to help.

"But God showed his great love for us by sending Christ to die for us while we were still sinners" (Rom. 5:8, TLB).

Love,
Dad

Something to Think About:

1. Define homosexuality.
2. What does God say about homosexuality?
3. What should be your attitude toward a homosexual?

It's Easy to be Envious

Dear Jim,

Many of us waste our time wishing we were somebody else. For me, it was Mickey Del Grande. He never knew it, and I wouldn't have admitted it to him. Everybody seemed to like this good-looking guy. Though he wasn't a leader, he was a person everyone seemed to like having around.

Sometimes we idolize people, and sometimes we idolize *things*. Every once in a while you mention something you really would like to have. Right now it seems to be a motorcycle. The 100's look terrific, and your friend has a nice one. Lately, you've only talked about it every *other* day!

There isn't anything wrong with wanting things. All of us do. When I see someone do good carpentry work, I eat my heart out. Often I look at airplanes and wish I could fly one. There are so many things I would like to do and have, that this page couldn't list them all. I *understand* why you want a motorcycle, a farm, and a weekend at Worlds of Fun.

It's all right to want things, but when envy enters in, it is a dangerous game. If we envy others, we might end up doing some strange things. Some people work themselves sick merely because they want what others have. Others even steal because they want more and more and are never satisfied. Envy could even change your personality.

Probably the worst part of envy is that we stop being thankful. We think about what we don't have rather than what we do have. Sometime, just for yourself, make a list of the things you have: the minibike, the stereo, the footballs, the trip to the Chesapeake for a month, sailing at Puget Sound, a trumpet, your own room.

You probably don't think you have much. Many boys do have so much more. But don't let that fact make you forget what *you* have.

There are a number of people I could easily envy. Wouldn't it be nice to be Johnny Bench? He was an outstanding student, an All-Star-catcher for Cincinnati; he

113

must be wealthy. Many of us wouldn't mind being Roger Staubach. He is intelligent, was a quaterback, graduated from the Naval Academy. What else could a person want?

But it is a waste of time to wish you were somebody else, or wish you had what they have. Work harder at being yourself. Nobody else can be you. And be thankful for all God has given you.

"A relaxed attitude lengthens a man's life; jealousy rots it away" (Prov. 14:30, TLB).

Love,
Dad

Something to Think About:

1. What would you most like that you don't have? Why?
2. Name six things you are thankful for.
3. How does jealousy and envy hurt us?

Hold Your Tongue

Dear Mary,

One of the toughest jobs in the world is holding our tongues. Talking about people seems to be the fun thing to do. Do yourself a favor—don't do it.

I like your example at home. You seem very reluctant to tell tales or name names. Rumors about who is stealing, cheating, or involved in sex and drugs make fascinating stories. The only trouble is, they do tremendous harm.

Even if a story is true, it isn't worth telling if it hurts someone. Read that again.

But I have to admit it's a lot of fun to talk about people. I hear rumors and I'm dying to know if they're true. Since I don't want to ask directly, I drop a bundle of hints, hoping someone will open up and let me in on it.

Are you suspicious that men gossip as much as women? You're probably right. Do Christians gossip less than non-Christians? We certainly hope so.

Gossip is like a good pepperoni pizza. It's juicy as a double burger. Talking about people tastes good. That makes it all the harder to control.

There is a true story about a doctor who lived in the Midwest. The town helped him through medical school because they needed a doctor.

When he returned everyone was happy. He was soon treating 30 patients a day. Then, sadly, a rumor started about his personal life. The rumor wasn't true, but everyone passed it on anyway.

Soon his patient load began to drop. Two months later he was seeing four patients a day. A month later the doctor left.

What a lousy deal! Many people were hurt because others couldn't hold their tongues.

Mary, have you ever been hurt by a rumor? You will be. It's one of the more dependable things in life.

It will feel like getting kicked in the stomach in the middle of the night. You probably won't know who did it and there won't be anything you can do about it. Usually, if you try to straighten a rumor out, it only becomes worse.

Keep a few things in mind. Gossip hurts, so don't spread it. Measure your words well—especially when they affect other people. Never try to get even for something that was said about you. Live a life that is honest and dependable, and it will be the best answer to gossip.

"... the tongue is a small thing, but what enormous damage it can do. . ."(James 3:5, TLB).

Love,
Dad

Something to Think About:

1. Has gossip ever hurt you?
2. What is the best way to react to gossip?
3. Why do we gossip?
4. Why should Christians avoid gossip?

What's Eating You?

Dear June,

A recent study indicates that people who are bound up inside with hate have difficulty thinking. When people hate they are less creative and actually score lower on tests. It can even make you physically sick.

Hate is much like a boomerang. We believe we are throwing it out to hurt someone else. In reality it only comes back to beat us over the head.

All of us get hurt once in a while. We can't help that. Someone is going to do something thoughtless or mean sooner or later. The important question is, how will we handle the hurt? If we let it turn into hate, we allow ourselves to be hurt twice. It's foolish to hurt ourselves.

A young man was shot in the back and became paralyzed below the waist. He said he had to decide right away that he would not hate the person who shot him. He said that life would be such a difficult adjustment now that he could not waste his energy hating someone!

It's true that some people do terrible things. You may have to avoid those people. In some cases there is certainly no sense in *looking* for trouble. However, we do ourselves a favor if we refuse to hate.

Young people are great. They seem to be big on forgiveness. They can scream at each other, argue, or even fistfight, but they usually become friends again quickly. That is one of the wonders of youth which I hope you will never lose.

Jesus was so refreshing here on earth for that very reason. Many people felt the only way to treat an enemy was to hate him. Jesus told them the best way to treat an enemy is to love him. That is a shocking thing to say, even today.

Many of us feel that when we are insulted or hurt, we have to get even. A few are actually afraid they will stop hating someone. That is why they think about hating them; they dwell on it, and even plan how they will show their hate.

Hate hurts many people. But, the one who hates is hurt the most.

Keep your fresh, happy, short-account outlook on life. When someone hurts you, shake it off quickly and go on with your full life.

"There is a saying, 'Love your friends and hate your enemies.' But I say: Love your enemies! Pray for those who persecute you" (Matt. 5:43, 44, TLB).

Love,
Dad

Something to Think About:

1. Has anyone ever hated you?
2. How did you feel and what did you do?
3. Why does hate hurt us more than the object of our hatred?

Does Marriage Make Sense?

Dear Mary,

Marriage has been getting a lot of bad publicity the past few years. Divorce statistics are high, and practically everyone on television seems separated for one reason or another.

You seem happily determined to marry. Whether or not you do, don't let the divorce noise frighten you. The situation is bad, but not as bad as it sounds.

Not everyone is getting divorced. If you get married today, the odds are 70-30 that you will stay that way and to that person. It's too bad that so many decide to break up. That represents a tremendous amount of heartache, pain and despair. However, it is not correct to say that *everyone* is getting divorced.

It's easy to get a divorce today. The courts are not hard to get past, and most friends and relatives accept it. They may not be pleased, but people accept it.

Even though divorce is fairly easy, twice as many couples still choose to stick it out. That tells me they are happily married, or at least working at it.

Marriage will probably be different for you than it was for your parents. More women work outside the home. Over 60% of young mothers now hold jobs. In most universities the student body is 50-50, male and female. Only five years ago it was 70-30, male predominant.

There are many changes facing marriage, and those changes are stirring the waters. Hopefully the waters will soon calm down, and the divorce rate will drop again.

Most of us need someone. That is why God created male and female. He made us to live in harmony, love, and sharing.

"And the Lord God said, 'It isn't good for man to be alone; I will make a companion for him, a helper suited to his needs' " (Gen. 2:18, TLB).

I realize you aren't about to get married tomorrow, so why bring it up now? I just don't want you to believe all the bad publicity you hear and see.

Marriage is strong, and marriage is good. It's a good choice.

Love,
Dad

Something to Think About:

1. Do you think marriage is a good thing? Why or why not?
2. Is everyone getting a divorce?
3. Do you know some people who did not marry that you admire?
4. Name two important attitudes you think you should have if you marry.

Non-Christians

Dear Jim,

There was a catcher on our high school baseball team who was a terrific Christian. He got along with people, was fun to have around, and yet everyone knew what he believed. Not a pushy person, he gained a lot of respect.

All of your life you will be rubbing shoulders with non-Christians. It's possible to be their friend and still keep your standards. However, it is sometimes difficult.

Some of the most respected people in the country are those who live the life of a solid Christian. There are famous athletes who get along with others but are still honest about their Christianity. One of the men I respect most is a Senator from Oregon who works for Christian causes.

It is possible to live and work among non-Christians without giving up your belief in Christ. It's also possible to earn their respect and friendship.

There is an important question to ask yourself if you have non-Christian friends: "Am I becoming too much like them or are they becoming like me?" If you are becoming like the non-Christians, the friendship is dangerous to you. If they are changing to appreciate your Christian outlook, the relationship is great.

Stay away from the guy who thinks it's cute to steal. Go slowly with someone who believes lying is the way to get out of things. Keep your distance from anyone who likes to hurt others.

I knew a group of young people who used to steal from a local store. They didn't steal anything they needed. In fact, they threw everything away after they left the store!

Don't let this pull you in. Only harm can come from it.

The same rule is also true about Christian friends. Sometimes they can drag you down to do things you know are wrong.

Jesus said we are "lights." When friends see what we do, they begin to understand the goodness of God. If we aren't careful, our friends will put our light out and make us more like them. Don't let them do it. Your way of life it too valuable to be wrecked by others.

"Don't hide your light! Let it shine for all; let your good deeds glow for all to see, so that they will praise the heavenly Father" (Matt. 5:15, 16, TLB).

Not everyone will be thrilled when you refuse to go along. That's part of the price you pay. However, many will respect you because you know where to draw the line and you stick with it.

Some of your friends may begin to drink beer or take drugs. That will add pressure to your life. What will you do? How far will you go?

It really helps to be a Christian. You have a standard to keep. You don't have to try something just because your friends do.

You're tough! You're tough enough to keep from being fooled.

Love,
Dad

Something to Think About:

1. Name a Christian you respect. Why?
2. How are Christians and non-Christians often different?
3. What is an important question to ask if you have non-Christian friends?

Getting Physical

Dear Mary,

Everybody wants an answer. We want a leader to stand up, and draw lines we all can understand. That way we don't have to make decisions. Making decisions is hard!

I can remember a speaker declaring that no couple should kiss before they get married. As far as I could tell, he was the only person in the room who believed that. Another "youth" speaker tried to become more scientific. He felt it was all right to kiss for a second, but if you lingered it became a sin.

We all get silly trying to lay down laws that aren't in the Bible. We become absolutely ridiculous trying to make laws for others.

It's like the youth group that ruled that no girls could go sledding in slacks. They thought it was more modest for the girls to go sliding down mountains in skirts.

The Pharisees would have loved all this nit-picking. They probably knew just how many fingers a couple could hold before it became sin.

There is no easy way to legislate personal morality. The Bible gives us a broad outline. Having a sexual relationship before marriage is definitely out. It is on the rise among teenagers, but that doesn't change the fact. The Bible tells us to avoid it.

Other decisions seem to be left up to us. Should dates hold each other? Should they kiss good-night? Most couples who date regularly probably do.

There is one guideline that seems to make a great deal of sense. Think it over for yourself. A couple seldom *retreats* in their physical contact. If they kiss, they will kiss again. If they hug and hold, they will do it again. And so it goes. We should never kid ourselves into thinking that we will only do this once.

The more a couple holds their physical contact in check,

the greater their self-control. The less they use discretion the more complicated their contact will become.

I have met many couples who have said, "I wish we had not been so physical." I have never met a couple who was sorry that they controlled their physical contact.

Life is not filled with easy computer answers. That's the price we pay for freedom. However, going slowly makes a lot of sense for a couple that is dating.

I think you understand and appreciate the problem. Take care!

Love,
Dad

Something to Think About:

1. What are some guidelines about getting physical on a date?
2. Do you and your friends ever talk about this? What do they think?
3. Why is it dangerous to be careless about physical contact?

Competition

Dear June,

It's fun to win! It's great to cross the finish line first or hear the teacher announce that you got the highest grade on the test. To come out first, second, or even third makes us feel good about ourselves.

But, the trouble with winning comes when you start to think you are better than someone else. All of us have heard someone referred to as a "klutz" because they finished last in the race. We have also heard of someone called a "nitwit" because he could not spell a word correctly.

We need to remember that everyone is important. Everyone is a valuable individual. A test or a race doesn't make someone worthwhile. The fact that God has created us and that He loves us makes us valuable.

People are not important because of what they do. The handicapped child who can never leave his wheelchair is worth more than all the money in the world. That child is important because he can love, he can receive love, and he is part of God's fantastic creation.

God understood the equal value of people. That is why He sent His Son to earth for everyone—not just the gifted, the fast, or the quick learners (John 3:16).

That really is a relief! When you finish dead last in a race, you can remember that you are still important. When you can't tell the difference between adverbs and conjunctions, remind yourself of what really counts. You are a person. People are valuable, and no contest will ever change that fact.

When the next whistle blows or the next test is handed out, give it your best. Don't settle for anything less. However, if you do come in high, remember that you are not a better person than anyone else. If you come in last, remember that you are still as good as anyone else.

Every day, win or lose, God keeps on loving us.

"We know how much God loves us because we have felt his love and because we believe him when he tells us he loves us dearly" (1 John 4:16, TLB).

Love,
Dad

Something to Think About:

1. Do you think competition (sports, grades, etc.) is emphasized too much at your school?
2. Do you know people with handicaps that you can help?
3. Why do people feel they must cheat?
4. What really makes us valuable people?

Nothing to Do

Dear Mary,

Sometimes it's tremendous fun just to be alone. You know what it's like to have all the family gone for the evening. The kitchen is yours; there is no one to bug you about the television; if you want to you can read quietly, gulp down a few cookies, and pretty much rule your own nest.

There is strength in being able to function alone. People are nice to have around, but not *all* the time! A well-balanced person can live with others, and he can live by himself.

I feel sorry for young people who must always find someone to bum around with. And they aren't too choosy about their selection of friends. They evidently don't half care what they do. Grabbing in the dark, they are ready to do practically anything with anybody.

Head for the middle. Gather friends, and be faithful to them. Have some friends who are extra special, and have many others who are just good to be with. But don't make your entire life dependent on company.

The person who can live with himself is ready for most any situation. Cultivate hobbies, learn to love reading, find joy in helping others. All of us have empty hours with little or nothing to do. Boredom is a central part of life and sometimes is healthy. However, the person who learns to constructively use his lonely hours has a better balanced life ahead.

Too much time alone can degenerate into loneliness. That isn't good either. The key to surrounding yourself with friends is to be a steady, outgoing friend.

The person who sits home wondering why no one calls is inviting trouble. Anyone who wants friends must take the initiative and reach out to be a friend.

If the question is, why doesn't anyone call? the answer

is, why don't you call someone? You do a good job here. When you want something to happen, you get on the phone and make it happen! There is no sense in pouting and wondering where everyone is. You go get them.

There is one thing we all have in common. All of us are hurting in one way or another, at some time or other. We all need each other. The person you are thinking about calling needs people too. If he doesn't need them this minute, he will need them later.

Living with yourself, and living with others makes a healthy personality.

"A man who hath friends must prove himself friendly; and there is a friend who sticketh closer than a brother" (Prov. 18:24, KJV).

Love,
Dad

Something to Think About:

1. Name three or four favorite things you have done within the last year alone.
2. Are friends important to have?
3. Why is it good to be just as happy to be alone as to be with friends?

A Tongue of Terror

Dear June,

"Call 'em up and chew 'em out." Some people believe that is the best way to get things done. They act as if life is one continuous fight, and they are prepared to bark, growl, and threaten until they get what they want.

We often watch heroes on television tell someone off, and we feel proud of them! Our hearts seem to leap, and we say to ourselves, "That's the way to handle them."

Maybe, but be careful. Most of the time harsh words only serve to hurt someone. They cause hard feelings and frequently do more damage than not.

The ancient writer of Proverbs wisely said, "Self-control means controlling the tongue! A quick retort can ruin everything" (13:3, TLB).

Don't develop a quick lip. Never prize the ability to cut someone down verbally.

There are times when it would feel so good to tell a person off. But does it really help? We try to hurt them, and in the process we might, but at the same time we are injuring ourselves as well. Instead of making ourselves bigger, chewing someone out usually just makes us smaller.

It's true that Jesus did use some very harsh words on a few occasions. He saved his toughest remarks for the Pharisees (Matthew 23). However, most of the time His words were kind, gentle, understanding, and considerate. His words had healing rather than hurt.

Have you ever been really "told off"? Do you remember the feeling? Did it hurt inside? Did your eyes swell? Did you feel anger rise up inside?

Are we sure we want to do that to others?

There are ways to correct wrongs. There are ways to insist on justice. Most of the time they do not have to include the tongue of terror.

Another Proverb tells us, "Some people like to make

cutting remarks, but the words of the wise soothe and heal"
(12:18, TLB).

I had the opportunity of meeting one of the most successful lawyers in the country. He has practiced before the Supreme Court, and his name dots many history books. To my surprise, he was a fairly quiet man. No acid tongue. No attempt to impress everyone. He was a person under control.

Keep the kind voice you have. Hand out generous words like medicine. You will heal many people who hurt inside.

Love,
Dad

Something to Think About:

1. Think of one thing you have said that you regret.
2. Think of something someone has said that hurt you.
3. Who gets hurt the most when we lose control of our tongues?

What Is Politeness?

Dear Jim,

When I was a teenager, I was privileged to meet one of the most famous men in America. Each year he was voted one of the most admired people in the world.

We spent a few minutes together, but he made a lasting impression. He was extremely polite. As an important person, he did not *have* to show patience and understanding. He could have been gruff and quick. But, not concerned about his position, he proved one could be an outstanding person, and be totally polite.

Compare that to the people you know who think they are cool because they are crude and rude. They seem to think they prove their manhood by being obnoxious. They insult people and act like it's a badge of courage.

It isn't so complicated to be polite. You don't have to take a course in manners. You don't have to know which fork is for the salad or which way to pass the peas. Politeness is merely being kind and thoughtful.

How do you make someone else feel welcome? How can you help them relax? What would be the thoughtful thing to do?

Politeness is always appropriate. We can be thoughtful of people younger, older or the same age as ourselves. We can be kind to friends and we can be considerate to members of our own family—even to brothers and sisters.

It isn't a sign of weakness to be polite. Rather, it is an indication that you are strong—strong enough to be nice.

Jesus covered the subject of politeness with one neat, sweeping statement, "Do for others what you want them to do for you. This is the teaching of the law of Moses in a nutshell" (Matt. 7:12, TLB).

A person can laugh, wrestle, hit home runs, go on 20-mile bike hikes, win water battles, play one-on-one, run cross-country and still be polite. The polite ones have it to-gether pretty well.

Love,
Dad

Something to Think About:

1. Who is the most polite person you know?
2. Do you think younger people are more polite than older people?
3. Do you think it's cool to be crude and rude?

How Mature Are You?

Dear Mary,

Young people and their parents seem to run on a gentle tension. On the one side, the young insist on more freedom. At the other end of the tug-of-war is the parent. We want to make sure you don't tear off more responsibility than you can handle.

Both of us have to learn that maturity is not an age. Maturity is a behavior.

Many young people ask the same question: "How can I convince my parents I am grown up?"

How do you persuade your parents that you are old enough to date? How can you get them to let you stay out late? How do you convince them you can go 100 miles away on a date?

The gauge your mother and I used was fairly simple. We thought you acted mature enough to handle dating. You seem to cope well with most of your responsibilities. Naturally, we think you could use some help in a few areas. We have mentioned these so much they don't need rehearsing. But, by and large, you keep your obligations. We're extremely pleased.

When we give you a time to be home, you almost always keep it. The exceptions are too few to mention. That looks like maturity.

So far, if we say some place is off limits to you, we believe you keep those boundaries. We don't spy on you or sneak around to make sure our orders are kept. To the best of our knowledge you keep those limits. You don't always enjoy the boundaries, but you obey them anyway. That looks like maturity.

We also think you have a dislike for lying. That's more valuable than golden apples. If you tell us you didn't do something, our first impulse is to believe you. We have no reason to distrust what you say. That looks like maturity.

Those traits didn't show up overnight. They are trends which you have established for years. They speak of your character.

Now, don't become bigheaded! There are many ways we still hope to see progress in your life. However, we are pleased with the general mold.

Many young people want to shortcut this. They expect their age to be evidence of maturity. Some believe size is the mark of growth. Neither one will satisfy.

You would like *more* responsibility. It is time you had it. When you receive it, will greatly depend on you.

Keep showing us how well you handle responsibility. We are impressed.

Love,
Dad

Something to Think About:

1. What age would you set for your children to date?
2. If your child asked to go away for the weekend with friends, what would you do?
3. Are your parents too strict, or too negative, or just right in giving privileges?
4. What is a good sign of maturity?

Other books by the same author

Counting Stars, meditations on God's creation.

My Magnificent Machine, devotionals centered around the marvels of the human body.

Listen to the Animals, lessons from the animal world.

On Your Mark, challenges from the lives of well-known athletes.

The Good Night Book, bedtime inspirationals (especially for those who may be afraid of the dark).

More About My Magnificent Machine, more devotionals describing parts of the human body and how they reflect the genius of the Creator.

Today I Feel Like A Warm Fuzzy, devotionals for small children which help them to identify and learn how to respond to their own feelings and emotions.

Today I Feel Loved, devotionals for small children, that build self-esteem.

Singing Penguins and Puffed-Up Toads, devotionals about creatures of the sea.

Chesapeake Charlie and the Bay Bank Robbers

Chesapeake Charlie and Blackbeard's Treasure

Chesapeake Charlie and the Stolen Diamond